The Day Underneath the Day

The Day Underneath the Day

C. Dale Young

TRIQUARTERLY BOOKS
NORTHWESTERN UNIVERSITY PRESS
EVANSTON, ILLINOIS

TriQuarterly Books
Northwestern University Press
Evanston, Illinois 60208-4210

Printed in the United States of America
10 9 8 7 6 5 4 3 2 1

ISBN 0-8101-5110-3 (cloth)
ISBN 0-8101-5111-1 (paper)

Library of Congress Cataloging-in-Publication Data

Young, C. Dale.
The day underneath the day / C. Dale Young.
p. cm.
ISBN 0-8101-5110-3 (alk. paper) — ISBN 0-8101-5111-1 (pbk. : alk. paper)
1. Caribbean Area—Poetry. I. Title.
PS3625.O96 D39 2001
811'.6—dc21
2001000129

The paper used in this publication meets the minimum requirements of the American
National Standard for Information Sciences—Permanence of Paper for Printed Library
Materials, ANSI Z39.48-1984.

TO MY FAMILY,
AND TO JACOB BERTRAND

Contents

Acknowledgments

Grateful acknowledgment is made to the editors of the following publications, where these poems—sometimes in slightly different form—appeared:

America
"Water's Edge: Impasto in Orange Madder"

American Literary Review
"The Magus"

Antioch Review
"The Hotel di l'Altissimo"

Chelsea
"Fireweed"

Christian Science Monitor
"*Étiquette et l'Esthétique Tropicale*"
"*Tuba Mirum*"

The Formalist
"Cancer and Complaint at Midsummer"

Gulf Coast
"The Philosopher in Florida"

Meridian
"Homage to William Carlos Williams"

The Metropolitan Review
"Imago"

The New Criterion
"Devon House"

North American Review
"Blue Springs"

The Paris Review
"South Beach"

Partisan Review
"The Apprentice"
"The Endless Cumulus"
"Sunday Afternoon"

Ploughshares
"Broughtonia"

Post Road
"The Effects of Sunset"
"Requiem"

Quarterly West
"Of the Garden Variety"
"Translation"

Salmagundi
"Arripare"

Sewanee Theological Review
"Poem"

Shenandoah
"Angling"

The Southern Review
"The Field"
"Minutiae"
"Stella Maris" part II (under the title "Vespers")

Southwest Review
"Complaint of the Medical Illustrator"

TriQuarterly
"On Privilege"

Western Humanities Review
"Exile"
"The Lesson"
"Unfinished Letter"

"Vespers" appeared in *The Best American Poetry 1996,* Adrienne Rich, ed., David Lehman, series ed. (Scribner, 1996).

"For the Sake of Tiger Lilies," "Ode to a Yellow Onion," and "To the Bougainvillæa" appeared in *The Writing Path 1,* Michael Pettit, ed. (University of Iowa Press, 1995).

"The Endless Cumulus" appeared as the poem of the day for June 13, 1998, at the *Poetry Daily* Web site (http://www.poems.com).

"Port Royal" and "Queen's Sapphires" appeared in *Will Work for Peace: New Political Poetry,* Brett Axel, ed. (Zeropanik Press, 1999).

"For the Sake of Tiger Lilies" and "To the Bougainvillæa" appeared in *American Diaspora: Poetry of Displacement,* Virgil Suarez and Ryan G. Van Cleave, eds. (University of Iowa Press, 2001).

I would like to thank my family for their love and support. For their time and encouragement, I would like to thank my teachers and my friends. Specifically, I would like to thank Geri Doran and Randall Mann for their help with this collection.

For a Tennessee Williams Scholarship in 1992, I would like to thank the Sewanee Writers' Conference.

And I am forever grateful to Susan Hahn for believing in this collection.

I

Homage to William Carlos Williams

I The Body

    You removed integument.
You palpated red fibrils,
    extracted breastplates,
exposed diaphragms.
    You saw the once rhythmic heart
still silent, again and again, in a pool of formalin.

    We begin the study of life
with our hands buried in the dead.
    This is how you did it
and how we will always do it.
    The body refuses the name *body,*
taking *cadaver,* meaning *to fall.*

II Corpus

Nothing could keep you away.
Not *Histology*. Not *Gray's Anatomy*.
You filled the margins of *Physiology*

with notes for poems.
Nothing could keep you away.
Not surgery. Not psychiatry. Not pediatrics.

Not the blankness of corridors.
Not the doctors you called teacher.
Not the New Jersey days silenced by snow.

Nothing could keep you away.
Not the little girl bundled against the winter sunlight.
Not the yellow wheelbarrow outside her window.

III The Body in Bloom

Geneva, the Lycée Condorcet in Paris,
the snow erasing everything . . .
how easily you forgot
the scholastic virtue of traveling.
You did not question the lizards

that ate contradictions
—both flies and flower buds—
the way *corpus* encompassed
not only art but the body
silent in the morgue.

You did not question
the truth of liver,
the truth of lungs,
the truth of blood when we are cut
so the body blooms.

Complaint of the Medical Illustrator

Here is the incision;
it will be your gateway to the afterlife.
Pull back the skin slowly.
The dead will tolerate only so much disturbance.

The blood you believed
surrounded organs and muscle is not here, is it?
See the liver,
it will bear you no fortune if eaten—

the ancients lied.
The kidneys? No, they were ignored altogether.
Now the thorax
is probably what you are most interested in—

the lungs, the heart,
that all-too-popular organ among your profession.
As you can see,
St. Valentine himself would not have liked it;

it is not attractive.
Now tell me, poet: will this be enough
to write your poem
about your artist, this Luca Signorelli?

Does *this*
really help you understand how or why
    he dissected
his only son's dead body?

Water's Edge:
Impasto in Orange Madder

Sunlight paints only the tops of the cabbage palms,
no, highlights their fronds with its fiery pigment

leaving the trunks to the shadows of their neighbors
that fall to the cloistered shrubbery, to the water:

a pond, a lake, a stream, we cannot tell—
were not meant to tell—from this framed perspective.

In this water steeped with weedy greens,
we find the heron, alone, its head tilted to the west,

and you know, of course, it pays no attention
to the sunset that is always arriving, granular.

But now even the heron is reduced to the background,
a young man joining the scene, taking his place

in a foreground beyond the foreground of this water,
his notebook in one hand, the other scribbling, quickly,

and you can tell, without ever seeing his face,
that his eyebrows furrow, his eyes squint to a horizon.

For that moment, his eyes do not dare leave the canvas
for fear the heron might, without warning, take flight.

Blue Springs

As if the sky during its emergence
—when it bubbled its way up out of the sand,
cooled and then sublimed into vapor
that blued the dank grey of the atmosphere—
left a residue of cobalt behind to remind

from where it had sprung into existence,
the water rising from this spring
appears unearthly, as only things
close to earth, born of earth, can:
its blue deeper than the heart of a sapphire.

Today, when faced with such a spectacle,
we have, as usual, only two choices:
the paralysis of awe, or the quick nonchalance
of acceptance. But what about the Spaniards
who came upon this spring before there was

a platform lined with inner tubes, before
there were wooden walkways elevated to slow
their impending rot, before there was a faux beach,
its sand stolen from the spring's center?
Did they run in with their clothes on

convinced this was *the* fountain of youth?
Did they laugh believing themselves
drunk, mad, asleep—dead, maybe?
That afternoon, late summer, we did not swim,
chose instead to wander out to the edge

of the walkway, not a word between the two of us,
only the wind. Unlike us mere mortals, the trees
had long since been impressed,
preferring, instead, to maintain postures
incompatible with the work of sycophants.

The Field

The hum of wood lice,
the way it
approximates

the frequency of C♯,
the way it is heard
only in close

proximity
to the rotting tree
that stands alone

in the field;
the wildflowers,
their colors, the fact

they are nothing
but weeds, their leaves
prickly like weeds;

the grasses, greens
easily separated
by the trained eye

into celadon, civette,
patina, veronese, reseda,
the common leaf-green

or shoe-bottom mold;
only with such detail
do I love you—

the paper-thin curls of bark
on our shirts, the dry grass
falling from our hair.

Millennium

The sun, barely risen,
threw spicules of light through the trees
to mottle three clusters of withered hibiscus:
we were silent.

At the time, who knew
a blackbird, its black wings glistening,
would perch on the *fin de siècle* to watch us
drink coffee and eat oranges.

I can never be sure
what it learned about us that morning,
but undoubtedly it reported us to its superiors—
everything in a green light.

Did they believe
that we were silent, that we did not kiss
or copulate or hold hands on the veranda?
Did they believe?

The twentieth century
will close like this: the two of us naked,
the blackbird overhead like the mind's ceiling,
like a darkly lit poem by Stevens.

The Philosopher in Florida

Midsummer lies on this town
like a plague: locusts now replaced
by humidity, the bloodied Nile

now an algae-covered rivulet
struggling to find its terminus.
Our choice is a simple one:

to leave or to remain, to render
the Spanish moss a memory
or to pull it from trees, repeatedly.

And this must be what the young
philosopher felt, the pull of a dialectic so basic
the mind refuses, normally,

to take much notice of it.
Outside, beyond a palm-tree fence,
a flock of ibis mounts the air,

our concerns ignored
by their quick white wings.
Feathered flashes reflected in water,

the bending necks of the cattails:
the landscape feels nothing—
it repeats itself with or without us.

Requiem

Again. Grey, the unsurprising slap
of cumulus and tumult, clouds
that never appealed to the naïveté
of Northerners culturing Florida
in dreams of steam and sunlight.

Grey, the state's grimmest truth,
grey on the order of silence,
grey to the point we call it beautiful.
Grey. Not the afternoon per se,
but the afternoon punctuated

by the punctuality of grey uniforms
marching away from St. Helen's—
how the mind dislikes the expected,
the children scattering
instead of remaining single file.

Grey, the inside of the church
denied the sunlit squalor of stained glass;
and grey, the old man's penance, the foam
on his hands as he scrubs the baseboards.
Grey, the nun's habit blown into a halo.

Poem

What we call rain,
    the water breaking
itself into smaller selves

    against a stone maybe,
better describes
    a sound, syncopated,

ever expected, unlike
    the sound of hummingbirds,
the clatter of their wings

    for the most part unheard.
What we call the horizon,
    the edge of the sea

from a proper vantage,
    is merely a line above which
we lift the images of birds,

    white tangents retreating.
And what we call personal,
    that abstract we attach to solid,

able-built arrangements,
    is quite often unimportant—
the sound and the line

    being everything, being
that which says *welcome*
    most genuinely.

Minutiae

Even now, whole patches of grass,
still white without moonlight,
testify that yes, the fire
consumed everything, laid down

white ash to mark its territory.
The sky is blue; the grass, white.
How else should I begin?
Should I begin with the walls

of the church, crumbled
under the weight of the flames?
Should I begin with the stained glass
now a spiculated pool of amethyst

come to rest against a metal beam?
Begin with the absent crucifix
or the tabernacle door wide open?
No. To begin is to start from zero.

Only then can we layer minutiae
upon minutiae, the whole picture
rising from the details, careful or not.
And so I tell you that there

among the rubble, feet away
from the ashen grass, I saw a vine
(well, a vinelike, weedy plant) growing,
pushing its small red petals into the air.

Fireweed

IN MEMORY OF AMY CLAMPITT

A single seedling, camp follower
of arson . . .

Follower of ashes; follower
of the bleached-out, burned-out
cascade of buildings, lotfuls

of whitened soil speckled with debris
let down by a gutted church
still aspiring to an ether-blue sky

centuries gone; follower
of scripts apotheosized into smoke,
notes lifted into air by flames

that all but threatened the entire lane
with the silence we call a bed
of dirt; follower of the match,

the instigator here and abroad,
the matutinal magnifying glass
focusing light into unwitting

summer grass, into cruciform twigs;
follower of the caveat
ignored because it was too small;

follower of the fourth-oldest dream—
the landscape burning and burning.

The Apprentice

Someone should have painted this room,
this studio already filled with shadows
eclipsing canvases in corners

where the grey at room's center
darkens to titanium black.
The oilcloth, nonchalantly draped

over chairs wooden and deteriorating,
gives them an almost classical air
only a student of sculpture could ignore easily.

Tonight, this captive block of marble alone
lights the room, and never before
have I feared it so greatly,

this material basic and yet so alien
I want to look away but can't.
Never before did I understand the Master. . . .

Here, in this room, a man lies
waiting to rise from this marble, unblemished:
Why have I sought the dead among the living?

The Magus

The pearls, mere reminders.
The ocean's rapid recoil, a signal.
The gulls appeared enormous

in that way only things from above can—
such is presentation of the sudden.
If only this were worthy of a frame,

the wooden gesture announcing
a moment past were cherished.
But it was too late for that, too late

to answer the surf's anxious *Why?*
too late to decline the continuous life
he had resigned himself, turning

away from the grave, that plot
being too familiar to so many.
Of course immortality had its price:

first his staff he had taped back together,
then the sleeves of his robe
he had reclaimed from the depths, then

the magic leached nightly from his fingertips
so that now his incantation for a storm
brought only a slight breeze,

a quick sun shower that frightened
only the flowers struggling in the salt air.
Now, showing his centuries, he insists:

This is the wind out of which I bring clouds.
These are my hands that gnarled though they be
when lifted to the sky bring rain.

II

The Footbridge in Summer

The shadow that is mold, dark and crusted
like the scum on the frog's back, has been encouraged
to run the railing and the rotting stump,

and I have pushed the sky out of the picture,
banned every cloud so as to free the lake
of the broad, slap-dashed reflections.

Even now the sun darkens my face,
darker still in this shimmering mirror
where herons see the hymn of the common bream

darting in pairs around a funnel of water.
What my grandparents left to me, the sound
of the Caribbean, its repetitions, is disappearing.

Ruckus of algae in late afternoon, ruckus
of the anhinga moving out over the lake,
the air beneath its wings sounding arcs across water.

South Beach

Memory brings us back to such a place—
the rows of photinia, each leaf a red flame
(blood-tinged, almost) violent in sunlight,
the sand not the white of the Caribbean

but the dingy mud-grey of south Florida,
the Atlantic sluicing the reef, whitening it
for seconds at a time, the sea sifting
through porous rock, patiently erasing it.

In a pool of standing water, clouds.
On the rocks, the sunlight on our backs,
you are looking into a puddle instead of
looking at the sea, its upside-down *V*'s

advancing. Curious, I look as well.
According to the physics of wind on water,
our faces wrinkle. I see my lips saying:
I will love you, I have always loved you.

Sunday Afternoon

FOR DONALD JUSTICE

Beyond the strings of water
clinging to the windowpane,

there were no cranes, just rain,
a sky blurred by wet glass,

a pond corrugated by raindrops,
and, inside, the smell of naphthalene bars,

a Victrola with a broken arm,
a spotty daguerreotype, a dusty crinoline—

O mildewed, seersucker suits
draped over vacant chairs.

The Effects of Sunset

Iron Shore, Montego Bay, Jamaica, 1974

At the edge of the yard, the grass thinning
to white sand speckled with the shadows
of late afternoon, the insects—waxy, black

heretics with beetlelike shells—could be found
avoiding the surf, and who but that small boy
could summon such a scream, that lion cub

in the desert, that whimpering Prophet-in-training?
In Judea, the insects bandaged the rotting wood
(or were they devouring it?), their slick

carapace without even a trace of sand.
One might say these insects swarmed,
but they were not bees, they carried

nothing sweet in their husks.
Exoticism, the late light, O summer—
a foot away, the water was dark, getting darker.

Of the Garden Variety

Before the first scalpel of light
crosses the red brick
that is never as red
as we remember; before
the air has lost the humid chill
that only a winter morning

in Florida can conjure,
the frost barely sharpening
the edges of grass
thick with neglect;
before the cardinal has time
to rise above this plot

in red garments reserved only
for such avian nobility,
Aunt Elizabeth would be sitting
in the garden, truly in the garden,
no chair, no footstool,
not even an old beach towel.

She refused to change her story:
she came out into the garden
because of the impatiens,
because they insisted so
last night, just after sunset,
as they began to lose

the turgor in their petals,
their pinks and purples
shriveling until they were
the fibers of an old dust rag.
And that was only the beginning.
When I found her there one morning,

her knees dirty, her hair uncombed,
I stood there and did not say a word.
She said, "Come listen
to the impatiens, come listen. . . .
Why are you so afraid
you might learn something?"

The Lesson

But this was not the first time:
the garish leaves of the poinsettia
scattered all over the lawn,

the hillside section of our fence
toppled, Father pacing the patio
just recently cleared of debris.

He complained, but was not alarmed,
his hands behind his back,
his air all nobility as he thought

about restructuring his army,
his household. How he loved this,
his chance to show he was lord.

Once, my grandmother, late one night,
her room flickering in the orange
but yellow glow of a night-light, told me

how a storm had torn down the villas
of the English princes—left only
the foundations, like sick, old cabbage

palms, for passersby to stare at—
but left the other houses standing.
When I looked confused, she laughed

and told me it was not important.
What was, she said, was how the sea
always took care of its own. Remember.

Outside, it only looked like disaster.
Inside, I was barely fourteen but pretending
to be a man, my hands behind me.

Thinking back, I cannot help
but wonder, to whom does the sea
now hold its allegiance.

Angling

So many books, and sunlight
bevels shelf after shelf with shadow.
Who remembers now the panic

of the broomstick at the death of the louse,
the ashes renamed *cinders,*
the dirty Ashputtle, Cinderella?

The ritual of leaves
dried to a crisp of carnelian
ends within the pages of a book,

ends on a day like this, a day
struggling under a blue weight of sky.
If I continue, if I choose to recount

how the robin stole fire from a child,
will you not wave me aside, quoting Crane,
"Fool, have you remembered too long . . ."?

But this is, of course, all speculation,
and you will choose, as you always have,
the stance of the reticent, the cautious—

silence, the one sound leaving your lips,
winter barely begun, and sunlight,
only sunlight, angling down the aisles.

Silence

This is not what I meant:
the glare of morning's grin, the seagulls
white like starched shirts,
the ocean air scraping the hill to our house
or the arch-lined walkway
to our now vacated veranda.

✦

Phaethon fell from the sky easily,
and what he felt—his chest heaving
like the ocean he was to embrace—
was not panic but exuberance or relief,
his father not as competent
at surveillance of the dead.

✦

The teacups, white as bleached bone,
delicate as bone,
lectured the saucers
already asleep against the linen tablecloth,
white and sterile as medicine,
a tea stain forbidden, absolutely.

✦

We will not venture down
to the sea today, the notion alien,
the salt air a familiar foreigner,
our shirts intolerant of a late-morning breeze.
At the table, Father sports a *Sunday Times* mask—
we do not feel the world or its blistering warmth.

On Privilege

The rampant cane fields rife with disease,
the ocean carrying only shells to the altar,
a beach left to penitents, their easy sweat
cursing the sand that brought an increase
in tourism. Could this scene be altered?

Next to a pile of seaweed, the ubiquitous gull
ate from a plate of dead things, rejections.
Up in the cane fields, sitting beside an anthill,
a young and foolish version of myself had once hid,
scratching in the dirt his tired testament, his will.

To my firstborn, I would leave the sea; the sand,
to my future love. But my father's grim shovel
I would bury under a palm tree, under tendrils
of clematis, its showy blooms filled with poisons.
One should not be alone in the cane fields, their evil

captured in their wide paragraphs, their evil refined
like sugar. At a resort staggered down a cliffside
to yet another beach, I sat one morning studying
the flowers of the crown-of-thorns, its bloodletting
worthy of an entire chapter in a book

on phlebotomy. In the air, I smelled privilege.
I remembered the cane fields. The years rewind
so easily for one who is a visitor in his own home.
The sea silences these false lines and mocks me
with promises of splendor and bright fish, reminds me

I am a fisherman, casting an empty hook.

Unfinished Letter

Dear Julie,
       I am dropping you this line
because I leave tomorrow for the Sound,
for Father's house. To think it will be mine
after his disappointment sleeps, the ground
too filled with discontent to care, the red
and silent earth a real and final gateway.
Imagine hell for him, no flames, his head
bared to a winter sky that spits its grey
and mottled disapproval down on him.
Think of our mother, she would not appear
to him because she had to learn an anthem,
her twelfth angelic march above the water
quickly approaching. Could her timid heart
withstand an afterlife with them apart?

Tuba Mirum

Et exspecto resurrectionem mortuorum.
Et vitam venturi saeculi.
—Requiem Mass

On a Monday like that,
you half expect the moon
to rise above the name,

to take its place in the sky
not blue but a grey silt
burying the Cumberland Plateau.

A bird's orange throat
could not resurrect sunlight,
not even a shallow flame

in such poor weather.
But the green flooded with music
so flawless in the wind

it made birdsong unbearable—
a boy, a virtuoso,
practiced his tuba,

Mozart, the lamentation
echoing down the arcade
in search of someone,

someone else.

Translation

The sea's reflected light
staining the walls,
the deck still dark
　　from afternoon rain,

an infantry of vines
overtaking the railing—
we were all talking
　　at cross-purposes,

commenting again
and again how the balcony
just wasn't big enough
　　for so much philosophy.

How many times
have we translated breath
into breath to avoid
　　speaking of *la muérte?*

And so, as if unavoidable,
someone said
that after Patroclus died
　　Achilles hated no one

but himself, the epic
of his life before him, alone.
Behind us, the crows bickered
    about interpretations,

the sea schemed
how it alone, light
or no light, would start
    countless numbers of poems.

Cancer and Complaint at Midsummer

Because the silence of the dead,
that blue expanse of sky about
to ashen here above my head,
is easily ignored, our tears
are blamed on flowers whitening limbs
of trees, the very air, with hymns
of summer pollen no one hears
except for women—old, devout.

And now, these humid months, dispute
them not: midsummer has no name
among the dead, no Latin root
to which it can be traced, no swarm
of conjugations to decipher.
So little left to write this summer,
my mind now weak in handling form,
which I still cling to just the same.

III

Broughtonia

IN MEMORY OF F.C. (1965–91),
WHO DIED OF AIDS COMPLICATIONS

But there under the dark eaves
of rain forest, we found *Broughtonia,*
its crimson petals aflame,
its yellow throat, veins hinting purple,

rising to a sanguine corolla surrounded
by sepals as crinkled as mourning crepe.
We followed a path lengthened slash by slash,
the islanders swinging machetes in front of us.

We were told how Broughton's hands trembled
when he sighted those orchids languishing;
as he sketched, his nervous pencil
exaggerated the crumpled edge of every bloom.

We too had learned to exaggerate.
That night in Montego Bay,
we told the others we had seen dozens;
in New York, we said hundreds.

Today, we might have imagined the wind
licking us back into the Gully,
our hands as uninhibited as those petals.
No. I can no longer imagine. I choose not to.

To the Bougainvillæa

How could I have imagined your absence?
In England, you do not haunt the streets.
Only weeds bloom in the cracks of sidewalks

to throw their white spindles on my shoes.
And what day could be complete without you,
your random reds, the way you climbed fences,

you, the rambunctious one,
the permanent guest of the stationary,
half-sister to the vines,

clinging where you were least expected?
In the window, my hair is white.
The islands did not prepare me:

how little I understood *white* there,
the waves of it breaking against the shoreline,
and everywhere bougainvillæa, bougainvillæa.

Aubade

Ocho Rios, Jamaica

This morning, the tide left us
nothing exemplary to peruse—
no whip-length kelp rusted with sunlight,

no shells spiraling point to rim
hinting that someone should listen
to their tired recollections of the sea.

Instead, what came in with the tide
were waves, silver-tipped, electric,
the sun reclaiming the island

from the dark hand of the Caribbean.
Who knows now what will happen?
Here in the land of two rivers,

misnamed because the Spanish
counted incorrectly,
everything revolves around water,

even the people, silent so the sea
will be more emphatic to visitors.
Alone, neither natives nor tourists,

we heard not the sea but the trees rustling
and continued walking through a shower
of methyl-orange petals, slowly.

Exile

Clothed only by the sound of the sea,
we stood naked on our balcony, masters
of all that lay before us, the green life

of the croquet lawn dotted again
and again by the cultured hibiscus,
its blooms the ready medium

of the master pointillist (read: *gardener*)
who now takes lessons from no one
but the river that has nurtured gardens

far more exotic than this, and on the sides
of cliffs, no less, as if to flaunt its virtuosity.
At that hour, even the handful of glare

left over from midday had to succumb
to the sound of the sea, its tireless percussion.
Sanded, our dark skin darker,

we had climbed seventy-four steps
into the heart of the palazzo, our suite
the necessary haven, the fort

we create no matter where we live.
And so, exhausted by the sun, we stood there,
two men among shadows, the sunlight

kept at bay by leaves, the two of us staring
at coconuts bobbing in the surf, strange skulls
trying their damnedest to remind us of nothing.

Étiquette et l'Esthétique Tropicale

Our mint tea cools slowly in this heat,
and off to the right, a single sail
cuts through the multiple shades of blue
I have seen only in the Caribbean:
blues and blue-greens deepening to indigo.

On the half-terrace, everything is more
than summer, a brine-loving tree
(complete with carnelian petals)
littering the walk with the withered pods
children sometimes use as maracas.

At this height, things fall away from us—
Look! Hibiscus cascading to the lawn,
the reds spilling over into pinks
then landing in fusions, inflorescence
a botanist would die for.

How easy to succumb to the tropics:
the flora, the white sand, the seascape,
the ever-present salt air of the casual.
At the mineral baths, virtually no one notices
the percussion of water falling down the rocks.

Devon House

Kingston, Jamaica

Lamps have begun to light as evening,
alluvial, fills every crevice in the courtyard,

fills Devon House, alone with its marble columns,
its verandas and esplanades empty,

the plantation gone, and the fields,
the courtyard a tourist attraction now:

glass ashtrays etched with boys
too large to be clambering coconut trees,

statuettes of women too smooth to be burdened
with baskets of fruit on their heads, stoneware

with doctor birds captured in the shallowest *bas-relief,*
key rings carved in the rough shape of the island;

and now even the hummingbirds are spoken of as jewels
where once everyone drowned in leaf-filtered sunlight.

For the Sake of Tiger Lilies

In a clearing, in a swell of grasses
thick with greens and yellows, he cannot forget
the ocean miles below the jagged rift,

the afternoons not laden with orchids,
afternoons not brilliant, overwhelmed
by the croton leaves inflamed with sunlight.

The old man glares at me, his voice tremulous:
the day is underneath the day—
there is too much freewheeling,

too much banter for the sake of posture,
for the sake of tiger lilies
drooping their speckled orange heads.

"The ocean is always waiting, boy.
An islander is never far from it,
always the sound, always the salt licking the air."

Ode to a Yellow Onion

And what if I had simply passed you by,
your false skins gathering light in a basket,
those skins of unpolished copper,
would you have lived more greatly?

Now you are free of that metallic coating,
a broken hull of parchment,
the dried petals of a lily—
those who have not loved you
will not know differently.

But you are green fading into yellow—
how deceptive you have been.

Once I played the cithara,
fingers chafing against each note.
Once I worked the loom,
cast the shuttle through the warp.
Once I scrubbed tiles
deep in the tub of Alejandro.
Now I try to decipher you.

Beyond the village, within a cloud
of wild cacao and tamarind,
they chant your tale, how you,
most common of your kind,
make the great warrior-men cry
but a woman can unravel you.

Stella Maris

I Matins

Journalist, diarist, poet—
age nine, I scribbled in the sand,
that slate cleaned twice a day by the high tide.

July could have been mistaken for November
but there were no uniforms, no frilly white bloomers,
navy-blue socks, patent-leather shoes,

no bells chiming the hour,
scattering rooks from the campanile,
no shadow of Sister Agnes pacing at her window.

July. Matins should be recited outdoors,
I believed, at the beach where the water is holier,
where the water is dyed by the heavens.

The birds left only the bones on the sand,
left the *ichthus* I had glimpsed on posters at school,
which reminded me it was lunchtime.

Because it was a pilgrimage,
we left during the fifth hour of daylight
like the children in our textbooks

marching off to fight with devils.
Not yet women but no longer girls, my sisters and I
marched behind our mother to the river

where a secret society of women holding white sheets
waded into reflections of rose-apple blossoms,
into the icy, black morning water.

We watched our mother drowning sheets,
then men's shirts, her back bending, straightening,
her arms lifting the white cloth into the air,

a benediction, her arms as fluid as water,
as fluid as a Chancery *f* written in fresh ink.
I would pull the white shirts from the water

—embarrassed at touching my father, my uncles—
and drape them across rocks to bleach in the sunlight.
Walking home, arms filled with laundry

sweet with the smell of the sun now dissolving in the hills,
I would remember my mother in the dark water.
I would pray motherhood would never find me there.

The Endless Cumulus

My soul is an enchanted Boat
Which, like a sleeping swan, doth float.
—Shelley

Red like the heart of a calcium flame,
the sun flickers at the horizon,

the sails of a clipper blown taut.
Sav-la-Mar: Shelley wanders the beach,

the sand flushed with twilight,
his skin bronzed, his hair blanched.

After a century of crepuscular skies,
boldly inflexible iguanas

with tongues the color of ginger lilies,
ospreys off course, young boys

fighting the surf red with seaweed,
cane fields uproarious in flames,

nights sticky with the scent of molasses—
again the dream he cannot help but dream:

the endless cumulus of the currents,
the ocean suddenly thickening,

the sun caught in the air rising from his lips.

The Hotel di l'Altissimo

Montego Bay, Jamaica

The wind ambushes the beach. Who is at fault?
Best to leave the coast, best to stay inland.
The Hotel di l'Altissimo's façade, stained by salt,
is all that remains, etched over the years by sand.

Don Tormentati thought this a prime lagoon,
thought he could lure Europe's wealth with coconut
water, pineapple juice, midnight bathing, a platoon
of gardenias, dahlias, rooms scented violet.

The moon gleamed like the china, bone white.
The breeze brimmed over with echoes of the steel band,
the nights burnished with flocks of seagulls in flight
while iguanas traced their testament in sand.

Soon there were guests taking photographs
at sunrise, favorable reviews in *Collier's,*
a troupe of lovers trying to outrun the surf,
gentlewomen in residence for years.

Touching the edges of charred concrete once lush
with relief, I believe the old man's tales: the hand
opening a window, throwing bottles of rum, a torch,
the smoke ascending, covering the island,

and then the islanders smiling as the Don walked past
with his head bowed, understanding that as sure
as there were goats at the roadside eating grass
he was no longer worth even the black of his signature.

Port Royal

Jamaica, 1960

Ignoring the local reliquiae—
neoclassical arches in ruin,
courtyards, their fountains toppled,

prados flourishing in prickle-weed, esplanades
no longer level enough to collect rainwater,
much less respect for the *Imperio de España*

tarnished by an islander's mock-British accent—
two fishermen returned at sundown.
Antiquaries themselves, these fishermen

schooled in the currents, the tide,
the tunneled limestone of the coral reefs,
preferred the graceful curves of the £.

At the landing, five children, single file,
marched away the birds like soldiers,
the learned lyrics escaping their lips:

Rule Britannia, Britannia rules the waves.

Queen's Sapphires

Port Royal, Jamaica

Here, Rome falls again and again—
the wind whistling a mock classic

through arches that can only feign decay
when compared with their Spanish cousins.

Once again, I have returned
to pace the crumbling sidewalks,

Port Royal the only remnant of Spain
on an island too devoted to the British.

Anxiety of crotons ripping up the esplanades,
sadness of palms leaning toward the sea. . . .

On every column, the determination of vines
to honor the jewels of a dead Spanish queen

with flowers as blue as blood.

Arripare

Discovery Bay, Jamaica

Under this cloudless sky, the sea is more blue
than green, the light binding to the salt air
with the force of molecular physics.

Surely Ixfœtay understood this,
Ixfœtay who watched the sea and sky
to warn his tribe about storms,

Ixfœtay, called Son-of-the-Sea in Arawak,
Ixfœtay, the man who discovered, supposedly,
that bauxite mixed with water could be used as ink.

Ixfœtay. I spell your name incorrectly,
the way Colón spelled it
in his logs filled with clouds and small Latin.

You must not have been well that day.
You must have stayed home while your wives
counted the coconuts, the guavas, the children.

Did you believe you could forecast
by the sky alone, that the clouds
were wiser than all the watchers before you?

Where were you that day?
Why were you not at the bay staring at the horizon,
you who had done so for twelve years?

Just so, a red cross, billowing in the wind,
rose from the horizon and entered the bay
under a sky that betrayed no storm.

Imago

I

The white tongues of the sea did nothing
to lure him, nor the white glare
of dissolved salt, the sins of seafarers past,

the lick and moan of tide under moon,
a great white eye open in the night sky—
if only it had been so simple, the sea itself

an open invitation, not the beryl-blue
sea serpents, sharks and giant octopi
swimming the *mare incognita* of the map—

II

The white of the sails stole his sleep; the white
of his sheets roughened like the hands of his men
scrubbing the deck in unfriendly sunlight,

the nights dragging their opposition to the currents,
the ocean breeze filling draperies, the windows clutching
shadows of leaf and branch landlocked under moon.

The priests on shore swung incense and chanted prayers
when, dreamlike, he had given the signal to embark—
the ships drifting out of the harbor,

Palos glimmering like a Spanish jewel,
each wall in the city a facet of *helios:*
arches, railings, windows, and roofs

gleaming white on an edge of blue,
the city focused into a point of light as if two angels
held a magnifying glass perpendicular to the sun.

III

The white of the moon held his gaze.
The white of the dead man's teeth held his attention.
The nights dragged his patience through black waters,

and the green meadow sighted was nothing more
than knots of seaweed in the Sargassan Sea,
the hills no more than cloud bank heavy on the horizon.

Like mist from an almost frozen sea,
weeks evaporated into mutiny,
the gunshot sounding one still dark morning.

The crew of the *Pinta* argued over shadows,
shadows that became land at daybreak,
shadows that spared him his life.

IV

The white sand assailed a legion
of foliage armed with hibiscus,
shadows alert against leaves.

Boys ran along the beach,
their cries like seagulls', like rusty winches,
their skin no darker than water barrels.

They ran past a colonnade of palm,
past an army of bougainvillæa
blooming in disarray, past the dark outline

of a papaya tree lying dead on the beach.
The glare clung to them like a nimbus—
he watched them from the ship,

charted their course, noted how
they leaped over unfriendly rocks
as they retreated from the vision of the *Pinta.*

As they ran down a dark corridor of trees.

About the Author

C. Dale Young grew up in the Caribbean and south Florida. He received both M.F.A. and M.D. degrees from the University of Florida. He practices medicine at the University of California at San Francisco and serves as the poetry editor of *New England Review.* His work has been published in *The Best American Poetry 1996, The New Republic, The Paris Review, Partisan Review, Poetry,* and *Yale Review.*

A Note on the Type

The text of *The Day Underneath the Day* is set in Sabon, a typeface designed by Jan Tschichold in 1964. Sabon's roman design is based on a Garamond typeface printed by Konrad Berner, who was married to the widow of another printer, Jacques Sabon. The italic was modeled after the typefaces of Robert Granjon.

The titles of the poems are set in Frutiger, a simple, clean, robust sans-serif type designed by Adrian Frutiger after being commissioned in 1968 to provide a highly legible signage system suited to the architecture of the new Charles de Gaulle Airport outside Paris. Frutiger completed the full complement of the typeface in 1976.

This book was designed by Heather Truelove (cover) and Maria A. Vettese (interior), set in type by Maria A. Vettese, and printed by Sheridan Books, Ann Arbor, Michigan, on acid-free paper.